RECONSTRUCTION

D1518981

Jamie McGhee

Children's Press®
An imprint of Scholastic Inc.

Special thanks to our consultant, Dr. Le'Trice Donaldson, Assistant Professor of History, Auburn University, for making sure the text of the book is authentic and historically accurate.

Thanks also to our sensitivity readers, Aaron Talley, a Chicago public school teacher, and Deirdre Lynn Hollman, Senior Curriculum Specialist from the Black Education Research Center at Teachers College, Columbia University, for making sure the content of this book is appropriate for school instruction.

Library of Congress Cataloging-in-Publication Data available

ISBN 978-1-5461-3637-8 (library binding) | ISBN 978-1-5461-3638-5 (paperback) | ISBN 978-1-5461-3639-2 (ebook)

10 9 8 7 6 5 4 3 2 1   25 26 27 28 29

Printed in China 62
First edition, 2025

Design by Kathleen Petelinsek
Series produced by Spooky Cheetah Press

Front cover: Like many cities across the South, Richmond, Virginia, lay in ruins after the Civil War.

Back cover: A freedmen's school, 1867

Find the Truth!

Everything you are about to read is true **except** for one of the sentences on this page.

Which one is **TRUE**?

T or F The 15th Amendment to the Constitution gave Black men the right to vote.

T or F President Johnson's Reconstruction plan was hard on Southern states.

Find the answers in this book.

What's in This Book?

The **BIG** Truth

Many newly freed
Black people turned
to sharecropping
to survive.

Black men gained the right to vote during Reconstruction.

The first Black members of the U.S. Congress, 1870

INTRODUCTION

The **13th Amendment** to the U.S. Constitution, which **abolished** slavery in the United States, was passed in January 1865. That meant that four million formerly **enslaved** people had finally been made free. Four months later, after four years of terrible fighting, the Civil War came to an end. Large parts of the country lay in ruins.

The city of Richmond, Virginia, was destroyed during the war. Like many Southern cities, towns, and farmlands, it had to be rebuilt during Reconstruction.

The Civil War (1861–1865) was fought between the United States, called the Union, and rebelling states, known as the Confederacy.

President Abraham Lincoln faced the seemingly **impossible task** of piecing the country back together. One of the main questions was how to allow Southern states to rejoin the Union. But there was hope. Under Lincoln's direction, America might be reshaped into a country that lived up to the promise of the **Declaration of Independence**, one in which **all people were truly equal**. This period of rebuilding was called **Reconstruction**. And it wouldn't be easy.

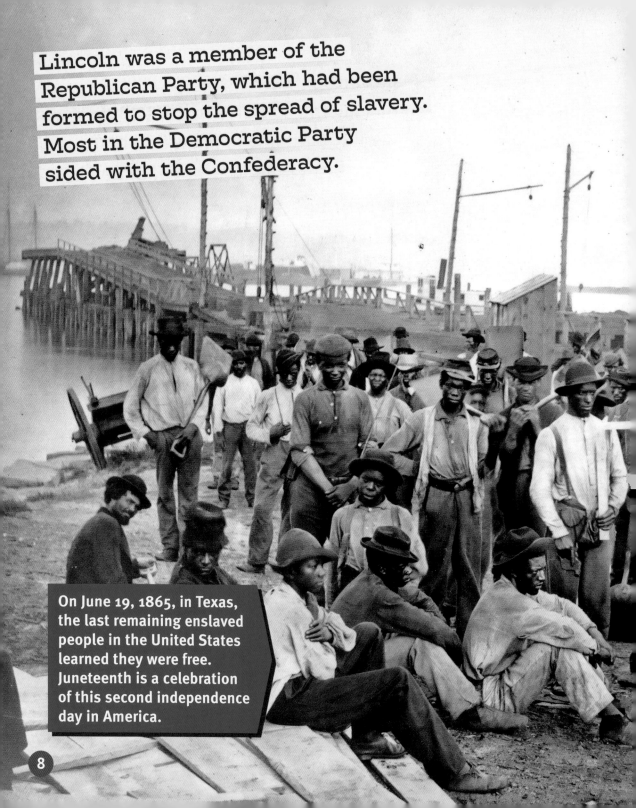

Lincoln was a member of the Republican Party, which had been formed to stop the spread of slavery. Most in the Democratic Party sided with the Confederacy.

On June 19, 1865, in Texas, the last remaining enslaved people in the United States learned they were free. Juneteenth is a celebration of this second independence day in America.

CHAPTER
1

The Beginnings of Change

In December 1863, Lincoln proposed his Reconstruction plan. It was called the 10 Percent Plan. In order to be allowed to establish a state government and rejoin the Union, each Confederate state would have to recognize the freedom of formerly enslaved people. And one out of every 10 men had to pledge loyalty to the United States. Many people in the North, including certain members of the Republican Party known as Radical Republicans, felt Lincoln's plan didn't punish the rebellious states enough.

A More Radical Plan

Radical Republicans created their own Reconstruction plan, introduced in 1864, called the Wade-Davis Bill. Before a state could be readmitted, 50 percent of its white male population would have to pledge loyalty to the United States. The state would also have to grant Black men

Radical Republicans like Thaddeus Stevens also demanded full **civil rights** and equality for formerly enslaved people.

suffrage, or the right to vote. Lincoln believed the Wade-Davis Bill was too harsh. He was eager to see the country come back together. So he held on to the bill without signing it into law.

The president has 10 working days to sign a bill into law or reject it. If the president doesn't respond in time, the bill dies. That is called a pocket veto.

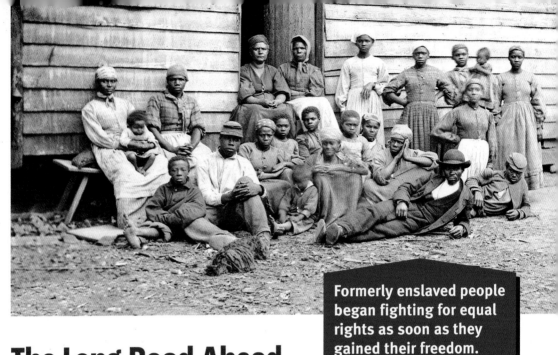

Formerly enslaved people began fighting for equal rights as soon as they gained their freedom.

The Long Road Ahead

After the war, formerly enslaved people, who called themselves freedmen, faced a hard battle marked by **racism** and inequality. They had to start their lives over with nothing. They didn't have homes for themselves or food for their children. Freedmen urgently needed jobs, but they had been forbidden to learn to read and write during enslavement. Knowing that literacy was a key to success, freedmen made educating themselves a top priority.

Freedmen Finally Have a Say

In March 1865, the U.S. Congress established the Freedmen's Bureau to help formerly enslaved people begin their new lives. The bureau provided food, clothing, and shelter, and connected freedmen to medical care and employment. Enslaved people had been considered "property" and couldn't get legally married. Now freedmen made their marriages official through ceremonies conducted by the bureau.

Education at Last

Freedmen who knew how to read and write taught others. With help from the Freedmen's Bureau, schools popped up all over the South. When the bureau did not have enough money for schools, communities of freedmen bought their own land, built schools, and raised money to hire teachers. More Black colleges and universities opened. For the first time in U.S. history, all Black students could pursue higher education.

Shaw University in Raleigh, North Carolina, was the first HBCU (historically Black college and university) founded after the war.

There were four Black colleges in the United States before the Civil War. The first, now known as Cheyney University, opened in Pennsylvania in 1837.

After the war, many freedmen changed the names enslavers had given them. That made it very difficult for people to find one another.

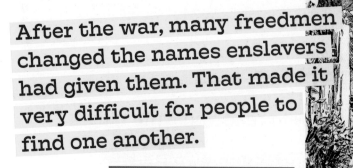

Sometimes enslaved people would be sold to plantations far away. Enslavers used this as a form of punishment or to make more money.

Reuniting Families

During slavery, families were torn apart. Parents, children, and siblings were sold away from one another. By the time the war ended, some of them had been apart for decades. There was no way for people to know where their family members had been sent—or if they were even alive. Nevertheless, freedmen tried very hard to reunite with loved ones. The Freedmen's Bureau helped. Some freedmen who placed ads in newspapers were able to locate their family members.

Impact of the Black Church

Even though Black churches had existed since the 1700s, enslaved people hadn't been allowed to worship freely in the South. Enslavers often banned them from using the same Bibles that white Americans used. Instead, enslaved people had to use a special version called the Slave Bible, which didn't mention freedom.

After the war, Black churches became the heart of many freedmen communities. They played a large role in providing education. People of all ages could attend Sunday school to learn to read. Black churches in the North also sent teachers into the former Confederacy to help newly freed people.

In years to come, Black churches would play an important role in the fight for civil rights.

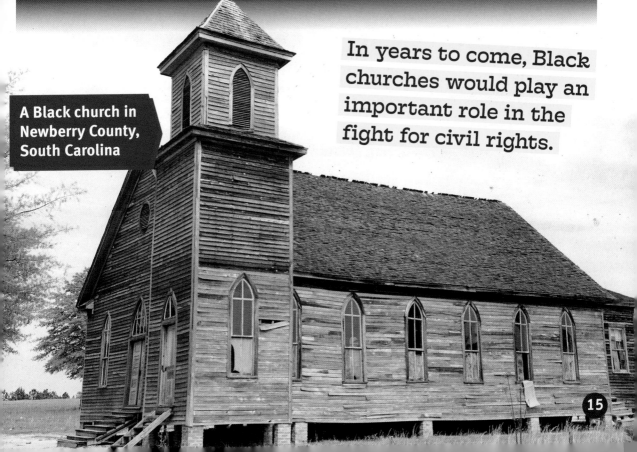

A Black church in Newberry County, South Carolina

Lincoln was shot by John Wilkes Booth, a supporter of the Confederacy.

Andrew Johnson (left) was a Southern Democrat who remained loyal to the Union during the war. Lincoln had picked him as his vice president to show national unity.

Roadblocks to Reconstruction

On April 15, 1865, Americans learned that Lincoln had been assassinated. His Reconstruction plan would never be put into action. Lincoln's vice president, Andrew Johnson, became president. Under his new Reconstruction plan, it was easier for Confederate states to rebuild their governments. They had to meet three conditions: uphold the 13th Amendment, pay off their war debts, and promise loyalty to the United States. Johnson did not believe Black people should have civil rights.

Black Codes

Johnson's soft approach to Reconstruction gave confidence to government leaders in the South. They passed harsh laws called black codes to deny freedmen civil rights. The codes forced many Black people into unfair contracts that kept them working in terrible conditions for very little pay. If they tried to break these contracts, they could be fined, beaten, or even forced back into unpaid work. They could also be arrested for not having a job.

Many freedmen who had been denied an education had to return to the same type of work they'd done when they were enslaved.

In many Southern states, freedmen were not allowed to gather in groups.

A freedman who was unable to pay the fine for breaking a black code could be forced to work for someone for free.

Freedmen and white people had separate laws and court systems. For example, if a freedman and a white person committed the same crime, their punishments would be different. Freedmen would receive physical punishments or the death penalty. White people would receive a much lighter sentence. The codes also barred Black people from voting or serving on juries.

Becoming Americans

In response to the black codes, Radical Republicans in Congress drafted the Civil Rights Act of 1866. It stated two important things: Anyone born in the United States was a citizen, and all citizens had the same rights, no matter their race. Johnson vetoed the law, claiming that it gave too many rights to Black people and **discriminated** against white people. Congress voted to **override** his veto, and the Civil Rights Act of 1866 went into effect on April 9.

An illustration representing passage of the Civil Rights Act

The Fourteenth Amendment

All persons born or naturalized in the United States, and subject to the jurisdiction thereof, are citizens of the United States and of State wherein they reside. No State shall make or enforce any law which shall abridge the privi-leges or immunities of citizens of the United States; nor shall any State deprive any person of life liberty, or property, without due process of law; nor deny any person within its jurisdiction the equal protection of the laws.

Neither the Civil Rights Act nor the 14th Amendment applied to Native Americans. They would not be granted citizenship until 1924.

Gaining New Rights

On June 13, 1866, the 14th Amendment to the Constitution was passed. Like the Civil Rights Act of 1866, the amendment stated that anyone born in the United States was a citizen, including African Americans. The amendment also stated that all citizens had the same rights, no matter their race. If a state didn't treat all citizens fairly, the federal government was allowed to step in with the military.

Republicans Against the President

In early 1866, Johnson declared that Reconstruction was over. Radical Republicans did not agree. They formed a special committee to oversee Reconstruction and started pushing for big changes in the former Confederacy. They also refused to let former Confederate leaders take seats in Congress. This put them in direct conflict with President Johnson, setting the stage for more fights to come.

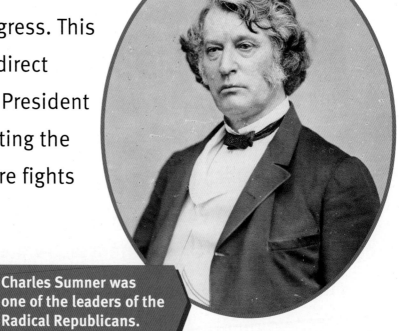

Charles Sumner was one of the leaders of the Radical Republicans.

Killings in the South

White Southerners were outraged that Black people were gaining civil rights. In response, they often used violence to keep Black people from exercising those rights.

In May 1866, a white mob attacked Black neighborhoods in Memphis, Tennessee, burning down homes, churches, and businesses. They killed 46 Black people and wounded more than 75 others.

In July of that same year, a mob of white men attacked freedmen who were peacefully gathered for a political meeting in New Orleans, Louisiana. They killed more than 30 Black people and wounded more than 100 others.

These **massacres** are just two examples of the violence that raged through the South during this era.

Seventeen massacres occurred across the South between 1866 and 1876.

An illustration of the Memphis massacre

The BIG Truth

A Failed Promise

One attempt to make newly freed Black people self-sufficient after the war was a policy known as "40 acres and a mule." Like many promises of Reconstruction, it went unfulfilled. Ultimately, the failure of the program made it nearly impossible for Black families to overcome poverty—the effects of which are still felt today.

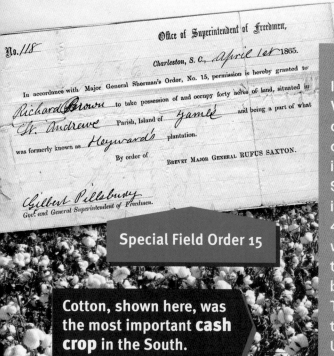

Special Field Order 15

Cotton, shown here, was the most important **cash crop** in the South.

A PIECE OF LAND

In January 1865, Union general William Tecumseh Sherman carried out Special Field Order 15. The order took land from Confederates in parts of Georgia, Florida, and South Carolina and redistributed it to freedmen in pieces of up to 40 acres. This wasn't just a gift—it was an attempt to repay people for the hard, unpaid labor they had been forced to do while enslaved. The plan had the power to help more than 18,000 freedmen families. Unfortunately, it didn't last long.

A CYCLE OF POVERTY

Freedmen farmers could not afford to buy land of their own. They had to rent it from former enslavers—sometimes going back to the very plantations where they had been enslaved. Freedmen also had to rent tools, buy seeds, and give a large share of their crops to the landowners. This system was called sharecropping.

Under this system, freedmen usually couldn't earn enough to pay for their basic needs, no matter how hard they worked. They got stuck in a cycle of debt and poverty, which made true freedom nearly impossible.

REVOCATION

After President Johnson took office on April 15, 1865, he reversed the order and returned the land to its previous owners.

The "40 acres and a mule" plan never officially included a mule.

Many Northerners moved to Southern states to help rebuild. Southerners viewed these new arrivals with suspicion. They called them "carpetbaggers" because of the fabric bags they carried.

In 1856, Charles Sumner, a congressman from the North, gave a speech criticizing slavery in Kansas. In response, South Carolina Congressman Preston Brooks beat him violently with a cane.

3

Big Strides Forward

Since the 1866 election, when more Radical Republicans were elected to office, they had enjoyed a majority in Congress. That meant they had the power to go around presidential vetoes. They could shape Reconstruction the way they wanted. One of the first milestones they accomplished was passage of the Civil Rights Act of 1866.

Radical Republicans were eager to punish the South. They were also committed to ensuring more civil rights for Black people.

These federal soldiers were stationed in the South during Reconstruction.

The Military Handles Reconstruction

On March 2, 1867, Congress passed the Reconstruction Act. This law allowed the U.S. military to enter former Confederate states in order to protect the rights of African Americans. The federal government also chose former Union generals to oversee Reconstruction in former Confederate states. They were called military governors.

Former Confederate states had to write new constitutions and allow Black men to vote on accepting them. The states also had to hold new state elections, overseen by Congress, and accept the 14th Amendment. Only then could former Confederate states become full members of the Union. President Johnson vetoed the Reconstruction Act, but Congress passed it anyway.

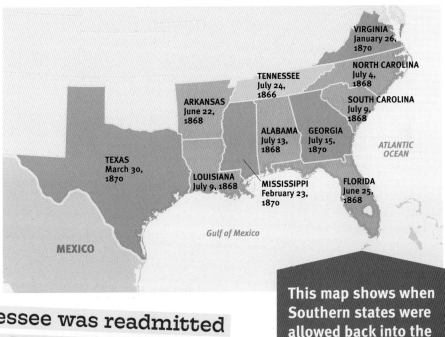

VIRGINIA
January 26, 1870

NORTH CAROLINA
July 4, 1868

TENNESSEE
July 24, 1866

SOUTH CAROLINA
July 9, 1868

ARKANSAS
June 22, 1868

ALABAMA
July 13, 1868

GEORGIA
July 15, 1870

ATLANTIC OCEAN

TEXAS
March 30, 1870

LOUISIANA
July 9, 1868

MISSISSIPPI
February 23, 1870

FLORIDA
June 25, 1868

Gulf of Mexico

MEXICO

Tennessee was readmitted to the Union before a military governor was appointed.

This map shows when Southern states were allowed back into the Union and military control ended.

Impeaching the President

Congress also passed the Tenure of Office Act in 1867. It said the president couldn't fire government officials without Congress's approval. The next year, Johnson tried to fire Secretary of War Edwin M. Stanton, who supported the Radical Republicans. As a result, the president was **impeached**. Not enough senators voted to remove Johnson from office, so he remained president.

After being fired, Stanton locked himself in his office and refused to leave.

Johnson's impeachment trial

The General Takes Office

In February 1869, the 15th Amendment was passed, giving Black men the right to vote. In response, violence erupted throughout the South. In November, a hero of the Civil

Under the 15th Amendment, only Black men gained the right to vote. Women still did not have that privilege.

War, Union general Ulysses S. Grant, was elected president. Terrorist groups such as the Ku Klux Klan (KKK) were on the rise. They attacked and even killed Black people and burned Black schools and churches. From 1870 to 1871, Grant passed the Enforcement Acts, which kept federal troops in the South to protect Black people. Despite the increased presence of the military, freedmen continued to suffer violent attacks.

African Americans Take Office

During Reconstruction, Black men overcame violence and other obstacles to voting. They succeeded in electing several African American politicians to local and state government offices. For example, in 1868, 33 Black men were elected to Georgia's General Assembly. They were called the Original 33. White Democrats, many of whom had been leaders of the Confederacy, dominated the assembly. They were determined to keep the Black men out of the state government.

The Democrats in the assembly claimed that the 33 had cheated in order to win their elections and demanded that their seats remain empty. After being expelled from the assembly, the 33 called on the federal government to step in. In 1870, Georgia's

In 1870, Hiram R. Revels became the first Black senator in the U.S. Congress when he was elected to represent Mississippi.

military governor removed many ex-Confederates from the Georgia Assembly and the 33 resumed their seats in the government.

From 1865 to 1877, more than 1,500 African American politicians were elected to office.

When Reconstruction ended, thousands of Black people made their way to Kansas and other states in the West in search of opportunity and equality.

The mass migration to Kansas became known as the Great Exodus. The people who moved, like the couple shown here, were called Exodusters.

CHAPTER
4
The End of Reconstruction

Reconstruction brought important changes for Black people in America. But by 1872, there was not enough money to keep funding the Freedmen's Bureau—and many white people felt that the 13th, the 14th, and the 15th Amendments, known as the Reconstruction Amendments, had done enough to help freedmen. The federal government disbanded the bureau. The progress made during the Reconstruction era was suddenly at risk.

Republican Rutherford B. Hayes

Democrat Samuel J. Tilden

The Compromise of 1877 put an end to Reconstruction.

The Compromise of 1877

In 1873, the American **economy** was in trouble. People wanted the government to focus on fixing it instead of spending money keeping soldiers in the South. Then, in 1877, Republican Rutherford B. Hayes ran against Democrat Samuel J. Tilden for president. Democrats and Republicans disagreed about who won the election. Eventually, Democrats agreed to say that Hayes won if federal troops were removed from the South. Reconstruction was over.

Denying the Vote

After Reconstruction ended, former Confederate states continued to create policies to block African American suffrage.

Literacy tests: Before they could vote, freedmen had to pass tests proving that they could read. However, they had been banned from learning to read while they were enslaved.

Grandfather clauses: Certain states allowed people to vote only if their grandfather had been allowed to vote. Black people were disqualified because their grandfathers had been enslaved.

Poll taxes: Some laws forced voters to pay a fee before voting. It was very hard for freedmen to afford the fee.

Violence: When these policies didn't work, people attacked or even killed African Americans who attempted to vote.

Despite racist policies, many Black men continued to exercise their right to vote.

Literacy tests sometimes included trick questions, such as "How many bubbles are in a bar of soap?"

The End of an Era

The Ku Klux Klan Act of 1870 had allowed the federal government to use force against terrorist groups. When federal troops left the South, violence sharply increased. Southern Democrats also formed "redeemer governments" in order to reclaim control of their states. They introduced Jim Crow laws, which **segregated** white and Black Americans and allowed racial discrimination in everything from education to housing.

Timeline: Milestones of Reconstruction

JANUARY 1865
Congress passes the 13th Amendment, abolishing slavery in the United States.

MARCH 1865
The Freedmen's Bureau is established to help newly freed Black people.

APRIL 1865
The Civil War ends and Reconstruction officially begins.

JUNE 1866
Congress passes the 14th Amendment, granting citizenship to everyone born in the United States and granting civil rights to every citizen.

A Disappointing Legacy

Eventually, all former Confederate states, as well as Southern states that had remained loyal to the Union during the Civil War—Delaware, Kentucky, Maryland, and Missouri, known as border states—passed Jim Crow laws. The laws kept Black Americans from accessing the same opportunities as white Americans. The system trapped generations in poverty and inequality—and would continue for nearly 100 years. The consequences are still felt.

MARCH 1867
The Reconstruction Act of 1867 allows federal troops to enforce laws in former Confederate states.

FEBRUARY 1869
Congress passes the 15th Amendment, giving African American men the right to vote.

FEBRUARY 1870
Hiram R. Revels becomes the first African American senator elected to Congress.

APRIL 1877
The Compromise of 1877 puts an end to Reconstruction.

People to Know

Blanche K. Bruce
(1841–1898)

After gaining his freedom, Bruce became the first Black person to preside over a session of the U.S. Senate. He was a senator from 1875 to 1881. Bruce's wife, Josephine, was the first Black teacher in Cleveland's public school system.

Rebecca Lee Crumpler
(1831–1895)

In 1864, Crumpler, who was born in Delaware, became the first Black woman to earn a medical degree. At that time, most medical schools refused to accept African Americans, and fewer than one percent of doctors were women. After the Civil War, Crumpler worked to provide medical care to newly freed people.

Martin Delany
(1812–1885)

In 1850, Delany became one of the first Black people admitted to Harvard Medical School, but he was forced to leave after white students protested his presence. He went on to become the highest-ranking Black person to serve during the Civil War and later worked for the Freedmen's Bureau.

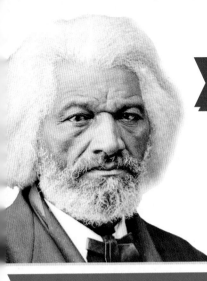

Frederick Douglass
(1818–1895)

Douglass, who was born into slavery, managed to learn to read and write while enslaved. On September 3, 1838, after several failed attempts, he escaped to freedom. Douglass served as an adviser to Lincoln during the Civil War, fighting for the government to pass constitutional amendments to grant civil rights to freedmen.

Abraham Lincoln
(1809–1865)

Despite having little formal education, Lincoln served as the 16th U.S. president and led the country through the Civil War. He also issued the Emancipation Proclamation in 1863. Before he was assassinated, Lincoln worked to pass the 13th Amendment, which abolished slavery. It was the first of the three Reconstruction Amendments that finally established civil rights for Black people.

Thaddeus Stevens
(1792–1868)

Stevens was a leader of the Radical Republicans and one of the most powerful members of the U.S. House of Representatives during Reconstruction. He fought for the abolition of slavery and played a key role in shaping Reconstruction laws, including helping to write and pass the 14th and 15th Amendments.

Eyewitness to History

Historians use primary sources to study the past. These are documents such as letters, manuscripts, diaries, photographs, and newspaper stories created during the time under study.

Enslaved people had to suffer the pain of being separated from their family members, who were often sold to different plantations. During Reconstruction, freedmen spent many years and tried many ways to reunite with their long-lost loved ones. Some placed ads in newspapers. Here are two examples.

ONE FREEDMAN in North Carolina searched for his wife. She had been sold to a plantation in Alabama.

INFORMATION WANTED.

Any information of the whereabouts of my wife, TECY RAND, will be very thankfully received, she formerly belonged to Dr. Banks, of Wake county, N. C., and was sold to Fabius Rand, in Clefton, Wilcox county, Alabama, about eleven or twelve years ago.

NAZERY HINTON.

Address Editor *Weekly Republican,*
Raleigh, N. C.

sept. 24—tf.

ONE MOTHER in Tennessee desperately looked for her children. They had been separated three years before the start of the Civil War.

A Mother of Twenty-seven Children In Search of Her Offspring.

To the Editor of the Banner:

Knowing that you have always been kind to the poor I desire to put this notice in your paper:

I desire to know of the whereabouts of my five children (colored), viz: Polly Bell, Grafton Bell, Jeremiah Bell, Lorenzo Bell and Fanny Bell. They lived in Dickson County when last heard from. I have made every effort in my power to hear from them, and having failed therein, am very unhappy.

We were separated in the year 1858, at which time we resided in Dickson County, at Bell's Iron Works.

I have had *twenty-seven children*, and now I don't know the whereabouts of *but three.* Very respectfully,

JANE BELL,

Formerly servant of Montgomery Bell and now at the Planters' Hotel, Summer Street.

True Statistics

Number of years Reconstruction lasted: 12

Estimated number of freedmen in the United States after the Civil War: 4 million

Number of African Americans elected to the U.S. Congress during Reconstruction: 16

Number of schools created by the Freedmen's Bureau: 1,000

Number of freedmen enrolled in schools by the end of 1865: 90,000

Acres of Confederate land set aside for Special Field Order 15: 400,000

Number of freedmen who received land through Special Field Order 15: 40,000

Did you find the truth?

T The 15th Amendment to the Constitution gave Black men the right to vote.

F President Johnson's Reconstruction plan was hard on Southern states.

Resources

Other books in this series:

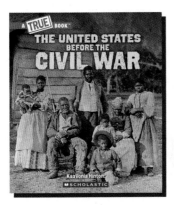 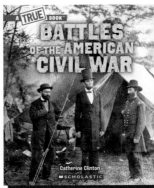 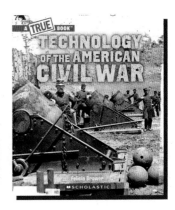

You can also look at:

Cummings, Judy Dodge. *Reconstruction: The Rebuilding of the United States After the Civil War*. Norwich, VT: Nomad Press, 2021.

Robinet, Harriette Gillem. *Forty Acres and Maybe a Mule*. New York: Atheneum Books for Young Readers, 1998.

Smith, Sherri L. *What Was Reconstruction?* New York: Penguin Workshop, 2022.

Wittman, Susan S. *Reconstruction: Outcomes of the Civil War*. North Mankato, MN: Capstone Press, 2014.

Glossary

abolished (uh-BAH-lisht) officially did away with

cash crop (KASH krahp) a crop, such as cotton or tobacco, that is produced or gathered primarily to be sold

civil rights (SIV-uhl rites) individual rights that all members of a democratic society have to freedom and equal treatment under the law

discriminated (dis-KRIM-uh-nay-tid) treated in a prejudiced or an unfair way

economy (i-KAH-nuh-mee) system of buying, selling, making things, and managing money in a place

enslaved (en-SLAYVD) held involuntarily and forced to work without pay under threat of violence or death

impeached (im-PEECHT) when a public official has formal charges brought against him/her for misconduct

massacres (MAS-uh-kurz) violent killings of a large number of people at the same time

override (oh-vur-RIDE) to use authority to reject or cancel a decision

racism (RAY-siz-uhm) the belief that a particular race is better than others or the unfair, cruel treatment of people because of their race

segregated (SEG-ri-gay-tid) separated based on race

suffrage (SUHF-rij) the right to vote

Index

Page numbers in **bold** indicate illustrations.

About the Author

Jamie McGhee has always loved to write. Everywhere she goes, she carries a notebook just in case she gets a new idea. Most of all, she loves to write the books that she wishes she'd had as a child.

Jamie grew up in the United States, but now lives in Germany, where she spends her time writing novels, learning new languages, and backpacking through the Schwarzwald. Say hi at jamie-mcghee.com.